Facts About the Fossa

By Lisa Strattin

© 2019 Lisa Strattin

FREE BOOK

FREE FOR ALL SUBSCRIBERS

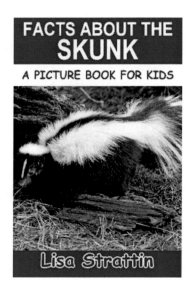

LisaStrattin.com/Subscribe-Here

BOX SET

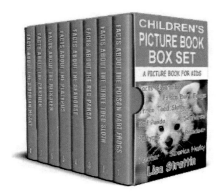

- **FACTS ABOUT THE POISON DART FROGS**
- **FACTS ABOUT THE THREE TOED SLOTH**
- **FACTS ABOUT THE RED PANDA**
- **FACTS ABOUT THE SEAHORSE**
- **FACTS ABOUT THE PLATYPUS**
- **FACTS ABOUT THE REINDEER**
- **FACTS ABOUT THE PANTHER**
- **FACTS ABOUT THE SIBERIAN HUSKY**

LisaStrattin.com/BookBundle

Facts for Kids Picture Books by Lisa Strattin

Little Blue Penguin, Vol 92

Chipmunk, Vol 5

Frilled Lizard, Vol 39

Blue and Gold Macaw, Vol 13

Poison Dart Frogs, Vol 50

Blue Tarantula, Vol 115

African Elephants, Vol 8

Amur Leopard, Vol 89

Sabre Tooth Tiger, Vol 167

Baboon, Vol 174

Sign Up for New Release Emails Here

LisaStrattin.com/subscribe-here

COVER IMAGE

https://www.flickr.com/photos/zoofanatic/8649104773/

ADDITIONAL IMAGES

https://www.flickr.com/photos/zoofanatic/8462177521/

https://www.flickr.com/photos/15016964@N02/5713713322/

https://www.flickr.com/photos/mathiasappel/34966166306/

https://www.flickr.com/photos/92306213@N00/3374089550/

https://www.flickr.com/photos/mathiasappel/19494129762/

https://www.flickr.com/photos/zoofanatic/8649104773/

https://www.flickr.com/photos/mathiasappel/19504925051/

https://www.flickr.com/photos/zoofanatic/8649106187/

https://www.flickr.com/photos/zoofanatic/8649103743/

https://www.flickr.com/photos/zoofanatic/15688259573/

Contents

INTRODUCTION

The Fossa is a medium-sized animal that live only on the island of Madagascar. The Fossa is one of the 8 ancient species found there. Although they look like a cat, they are thought to be descended from the Mongoose.

BEHAVIOR

The Fossa is a solitary mammal that does most of their prowling and hunting for food at night while sleeping most of the daylight hours. They live high in the trees but are known to come down to the ground to hunt as well. If food becomes scarce, they will come out more during the day to find food.

APPEARANCE

The Fossa is the largest predator on land in Madagascar. Their tail is about as long as the rest of their body and helps them to keep their balance while leaping around in the trees. They have short dark brown or red fur and a cat-like head. Although if you look at a picture of a Mongoose, you will see that their head looks like the Mongoose too! They have claws that they can retract just like the housecat.

REPRODUCTION

Fossas mate during September and October. The female is pregnant for about 3 months, and usually has 2 cubs in a litter. Like kittens, they are born with their eyes closed and don't open them until they are 2 to 3 weeks old. They can eat solid foods at about 12 weeks old, but continue to nurse from the mother for another month or so after that. They are fully grown at about 2 years of age and can mate at about 4 years old.

LIFE SPAN

The average lifespan of a Fossa is between 15 and 20 years.

SIZE

The adult Fossa reaches about 24 to 32 inches long and can weigh up to 30 pounds.

HABITAT

The Fossa needs forested areas where they can live in the trees and find plenty of food to eat.

DIET

The Fossa eats other animals in the forested areas of the island of Madagascar. They eat a lot of Lemurs! They also eat lizards, rodents, frogs, reptiles and birds. Since they are fast and stealthy, anything small enough that lives in the trees or down on the ground in their territory is a ready food source.

ENEMIES

The only natural predator to the Fossa is the occasional Crocodile. Of the animals on the island, the Fossa is the main predator, so doesn't face threats of other animals.

SUITABILITY AS PETS

Even though the Fossa looks like a cat, it is not a suitable pet. They are a wild animal, and live in the trees, so there isn't much of a chance that you could have a good habitat for one at your house. There are some kept in captivity in zoos, so you might check your local zoo to see if they have some you could watch up close.

COLOR ME

COLOR ME

COLOR ME

COLOR ME

COLOR ME

COLOR ME

COLOR ME

COLOR ME

COLOR ME

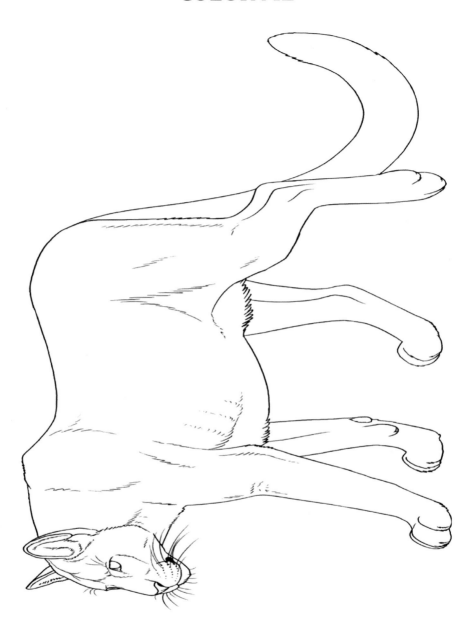

Please leave me a review here:

LisaStrattin.com/Review-Vol-322

For more Kindle Downloads Visit Lisa Strattin Author Page on Amazon Author Central

amazon.com/author/lisastrattin

To see upcoming titles, visit my website at LisaStrattin.com– most books available on Kindle!

LisaStrattin.com

FREE BOOK

FOR ALL SUBSCRIBERS – SIGN UP NOW

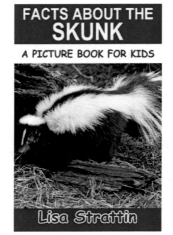

LisaStrattin.com/Subscribe-Here

LisaStrattin.com/Facebook

LisaStrattin.com/Youtube